# A MATTER OF INCLUSION

*POEMS*

## CHAD NORMAN

**Edited by Tendai R. Mwanaka**

Mwanaka Media and Publishing Pvt Ltd,
Chitungwiza Zimbabwe
*
*Creativity, Wisdom and Beauty*

Publisher: *Mmap*
Mwanaka Media and Publishing Pvt Ltd
24 Svosve Road, Zengeza 1
Chitungwiza Zimbabwe
mwanaka@yahoo.com
mwanaka13@gmail.com
https://www.mmapublishing.org
www.africanbookscollective.com/publishers/mwanaka-media-
and-publishing
https://facebook.com/MwanakaMediaAndPublishing/

Distributed in and outside N. America by African Books
Collective
orders@africanbookscollective.com
www.africanbookscollective.com

ISBN: 978-1-77921-334-1
EAN: 9781779213341

DISCLAIMER
All views expressed in this publication are those of the author
and do not necessarily reflect the views of *Mmap*.

ii

# ACKNOWLEDGEMENTS

The following poems have appeared in the following publications:

We Let them Do it: *Azahar Revista Poetica, #105 (Spain)*; Romerica, The Battered One, Life In Quarantine, *Stanford University, California; The Typescript, Boston, MA;* Further Observations Of A Furious Blend: *Ablucionistas, Mexico* and *Nova Scotia Advocate;* A Matter Of Inclusion: *Atunis Galaktika Poetike, Belgium; Ivy Magazine, Letras Del Mund, Mexico. Translated in Spanish;* My Part, My Place: *Chinese And Foreign Literature,!st Place in World Newspaper & TV Competition, China; Dreich Magazine, Scotland;* There Is So Much Room: *Trinity Review, Toronto, Canada;* The People Are Waves: *I Am Not A Silent Poet, Spain;* The Broken Garden: *Poesis International, Romania, translated into Romanian; Poet Of The Time Repblic, Africa; I Am Not A Silent Poet, Spain;* The Precarious Admission: *Spillwords, New York City;* The Expanse Of Inclusion: *Poesis International, Romania, translated into Romanian; Adwa-Almadena, Syria; Dovetales, Scotland;* The Erosion Of Borders: *Miletus, USA and Turkey; Ivy Magazine, Letras Del Mund, translated into Spanish;* The Lighting Of A Candle: *Poetry And Settled States For All Anthology, Poesis International, Romania, translated into Romanian; Poet Of The Time Republic, Africa;* A Nationwide Plea, Or Request For Fewer Misled Borders: *Ivy Magazine, Letras Del Mund, Mexico. Translated into Spanish;* Ending With The Skin: *Ivy Magazine, Letras Del Mund, Mexico. Translated into Spanish; Promotion of Chinese Literature And Foreign Literature, China; Queen's Quarterly, Canada;* The Contamination Of Red: *Ivy Magazine, Letras Del Mund, Mexico. Translated into Spanish; The Kist Of Thistles Anthology, Culture Matters, Ireland;* Learning To Be An Older Man: *Dreich Magazine, Scotland;* Where The Path Is Melting: *Poet Of The Time Republic, Africa; Adwa-Aladema, Syria; Second Name For Earth Is Peace anthology, Africa;* A Raven's Sermon: *Live Encounters. 10th Anniversary Edition, Phillipines;* The Good In Us: *Bangor Literay magazine, Bangor, Ireland;* Depiction:

*Imspired, England; Nova Scotia Advocate;* I Speak: *Backstory, Australia;* I Speak For: *Backstory, Australia;* I Speak Against: *I Am Not A Silent Poet, Spain;* The Rights Of One: *Poesis International, Romania. Translated into Romanian. Black Lives Matter Anthology, Leicester, UK;* The Smashed Cello: *Poesis International, Romania. Translated into Romanian; The Elixir magazine, Yemen;* The Proof Is In The Puppeteers: *Armagan, Bosnia; Strands Literary Sphere, India;* Bandaid On The Sidewalk: *The Elixir Magazine, Yemen; I Am Not A Silent Poet, Spain;* Declaration For The Banished: *Poesis International, Romania. Translated into Romanian; I Am Not A Silent Poet, Spain;* The Flagless Flagpole: *Poet Of The Time Republic, Africa; Live Encounters, 10th Anniversary Edition, Phillipines; Second Name For Earth Is Peace anthology, Africa;* The Silence of Tiles: *Truro Daily News, Nova Scotia, Canada;* Watering The Flag: *The Blue Nib, England;* Messiah For The Misled: *Nationalism Anthology, Africa vs North America Vol 2, Zimbabwe, Atunis, Belgium; Culture Matters, Ireland; Poesis International, Romania;* Megaphones In A Parade: *N. S. Advocate, Canada;* Who I Move Beside: *N. S. Advocate, Canada;* The Arms of A Palestinian Woman: *Bangor Literary Magazine, Ireland;* The Important Mistakes: *Azahar Revista Poetica, #107, Spain;* Woman Sitting In A Chair Wearing A White Poppy: *Blank Spaces Magazine, Canada; Revista Poetica Azahar, Spain;* Cling: *Armagan, Iran; Black Spaces.*

# OTHER BOOKS BY CHAD NORMAN

On The Urban Prairie & Other Shorter Poems, 1986
And If A Man Be Divided, 1991
Lives Of The Year, 1994
Standing In The Corner, 1995
The Breath Of One, 1997
What The Wind Brings, 1999
These Are My Elders, 2001
The Kulling, 2001
The Soft Furnace, 2006
Going Mad For The Love Of Sanity, 2008
There Is Music In The Word Impeachment, 2009
Ants On The Rainbow: Poems To, For, And About Children, 2010
Hugging The Huge Father, 2011
Hugging The Huge Father, Expanded Version 2012
Masstown, 2013
Learning To Settle Down, 2015
Selected & New Poems, 2017
Squall: Poems In The Voice of Mary Shelley, 2020
Simona: A Celebration Of The S.P.C.A., 2021

## Dedication

*for all my grandchildren, may the world they inherit be wiser than mine, more understanding and loving of the people these poems honour.*

# TABLE OF CONTENTS

# INTRODUCTION

I have been writing and publishing poetry for 40 years, during which time I have lived in various places in Canada, including on both west and east coasts. During this time, I have had the privilege of witnessing the changing face, and faces, of Canada. I have had the opportunity to work, often in warehouses and factories, with Canadians with roots all over the world, including Indigenous Canadians, new immigrants, and those whose parents or grandparents chose to make Canada their home. I currently live in Truro, Nova Scotia, which continues to grow, enriched by the businesses and cultures and cuisines introduced by new arrivals every day. (For nine years I have hosted the annual RiverWords Poetry and Music Festival which showcases artists from a variety of cultural backgrounds.) My poetry has always delved into those places where the personal and public intersect. At this stage in my career, I could not take myself seriously as a writer if I were not exploring and celebrating the changes I see in my community.

The goal of this current project is to educate myself: I want to understand what it is like to find one's home in Canada, whether it is for economic or political reasons, or having to flee violence. I want to come as close to understanding as possible, and as a white man who has lived in Canada his whole life, I can only do that by asking questions, and by connecting my personal experience with that of others. This is what my poems are about.

For example, in the poem "Cling," which was recently published in Armagan Magazine in Tehran, Iran, I observed one last leaf clinging to a tree at the same moment I encountered a young immigrant mother in my community Truro. I took the risk of asking her about her experience, and had an amazing conversation; the poem is the result of the insight I was privileged to receive.

My work has always been, and continues to be well-received abroad. My poems have been published all over the world, including China, India, Iran, the Philippines, Turkey, Albania, Spain, Ireland, etc. Many of them have been translated into other languages. In recent years, I have had the opportunity to tour Denmark, Sweden, Ireland and the U.K. Audiences have been keen to learn about and celebrate Canadian poetry. They are also interested in learning about Canada's experience with immigration and multiculturalism. They want to learn about the process of inclusion, about the problems and successes alike. It is, of course, paramount that they hear the voices of those immigrants themselves, a process I fully support and celebrate. But I believe voices like mine can also contribute constructively and uniquely to that conversation.

Chad Norman
January,                                                           2022

# WE LET THEM DO IT

Them.
Them?
Them!
Them...

I am invested
in a way I stand by
knowing who is the "them"
is vital, is a hand
held out to my life,
my heart, my mind,
who I am
invested in loving "them",
who I am
when seated alone
knowing my country,
how huge it is,
how loving it can be,
how there is nothing wrong
with being a welcome mat
when standing with others
I have no idea
have been born here,
here in Canada.

We let them do it...
convincing us it is patriotic,
it is what we should do,
it is our right to take
such a stance knowing so little.

We let them do it.
Sway our minds to be
on the side of best described
as Exclusion, being threatened
in some misled way,
a way limiting to what we
as Canadians are seen as,
being open, always remembering
we may just be related to
another family forced to
be hopeful with a choice
to absolutely be convinced
it is time to leave one home
to seek another so far away,
another so full of sensible
unique minds & hearts,
alive in what can be said
to be the *real* Canadian,
the opposition ready to lead
the choice we are all about.

Think about it...
who makes they
the Them?

## ROMERICA, THE BATTERED ONE
*for Jay Hamburger*


She.
Her.
A nation is not a woman...
not even close.

But in all those songs
and even the odd poem
the writers of that time
saw you as one.

I never liked it...
women shouldn't be womanized
for a song or any poem...
as far as a nation
many choose to live too...
it being simply a nation.

No woman really loathes life,
life being her fellow species.

Life is
all those trying to be alive
no matter where the borders
have said you can be found,
borders aren't about all of us
staying away from political punches.
All the helpful forces like DACA,
movements of families and dreams

3

belong to you, Romerica,
nothing taken away
as the present stretches beyond
the sightless, the visionless,
who you will shake off soon.

Yet I look closely
and see them
holding the swabs ready to test,
strong in the hallways of hospitals,
wiping the mouths of dying mothers,
picking, picking, the food you eat.

Romerica, the battered one,
taking beating after beating,
all to see, all of your people
infected or not, allowing it,
so many marches onward,
what about for one needed now?

The one on behalf of those living
behind the skin of many colours
afraid to step outside
where the street leads to a dock,
or perhaps a beach where
no cages are found in the sand
and fears wear off for smiles you want
on the faces of those arriving
who have given up homelands,
to show up in the mornings
or if needed to take on a night-shift.

You are the battered one
on knees with too many bruises
and eyes blackened
by centuries of choices
to erect statues meant for a past
you have held to your misled head
where a house full of conning men
try to lead, try to be whiter than white,
a cause the rest of the world
watches you withstand, almost
as if it is deserved, hoping
the beatings will open cell-doors.

Somehow there will be sentences
ordered by a new, sane justice
one I want, one I wish for,
a justice about the need our
entire world will finally provide
but more for you, Romerica,
to begin what may prevent
the crumbling caused by fists
owned by the comical politicos
standing on you, full of energy
all about a need to hate,
disregard, drag along
no matter how heavy
or unnecessary for you
to open to a suppressed future.

People know what they see
and silence has never worked,
time has come for you
to seek help, if you do

don't be surprised by the colour
of who brings it on,
takes away all the attacks and
perhaps, further racist possibilities.

She.
Her.
Lady said to be fat.
A remedy won't be in a vaccination...
not even close.

A country is not a victim...
wake up, please, Romerica,
find the embrace for all of
who you are, who will be
what you become when voters
have the say,  healing of that oval room
comes, like leaves as they begin
to change their historic colours.

# FURTHER OBSERVATIONS OF A FURIOUS BLEND

1

Mostly a man,
carrying a gigantic gun,
death and disease
causing a certain patriotism.

Parading the dreams of thieves
he stands where he wants to
before settling on a position among
who he believes are trusty brothers.

The gigantic gun seems to carry him
even though his shoulder submits,
at times it outsizes how small
he seems to be, even though the media
has a specific size for him,
a choice several stations select
to pass off a threat I dismiss.

How he turns up on the steps
or poised like a soldier in halls
of so many government buildings--
I am sure you have seen him there.
Seemingly so confident, unalone
and unafraid, the gigantic gun
falling over him like a fashion
chosen by those brothers,  everything
to do with a white Romerica.

Something has stolen the man inside
all the appearances and marching
brings nothing more than he had...
the gun will never be big enough
in order for those trusted brothers
to be men too, something so seen,
so obvious, let his longing out
to be as white as his willing hatred.

2

Mostly a woman
lifting a legible slogan,
birth and burden
write: "Caring For One Another is Right!"

Hearing the dreams of marchers
a question keeps being asked,
"Is this how she'll be a part of change?"
Over there beside the burnt cop-shop,
over there beside all the murdered
black loved ones, stolen from a
family somewhere, to be left in
a cemetery to be alive forever.

Her voice is from all the voices
I hear in the marches, in
my other family members
who choose to carry the colour of skin

in other than the weight on faces,
carrying it on placards and signs
made for the day it could be seen
and able to speak, the colour of,
the skin of, all of them like a
harmony, like a collection, like
what she says about a country,
a house so sick, a house so white,
yeah, you know it, where traitors
and liars enjoy success, all being
part of what so many eyes see.

A woman has taken back sanity
what can be defined as a "return-
to-sender" put in rising fists,
and then when the streets want
more voices, more of other
than the furious blend, it is good,
it is all about how what is going on
out there in Romerica, brought down
by a red-headed misleader, put in place
by an addict in love with the mix
he needs daily: fraud, incarceration,
racism, cheating, infamous addictions
labelled a presidency, the reason
to walk with her dealing in
some further observations, lucrative
when another election brings reprieve,
points to a way out and a way in,
a future less eager to be a mystery.

# A MATTER OF INCLUSION

Skin,
the colour of,
enough to
keep us
a devolved species.

Our planet
is waiting for otherwise,
have you noticed
how patient
it remains?

Really,
borders mean little
in certain minds,
may those minds
become our leaders.

A matter of inclusion
I will share with you,
Canada has no need
for any lack of possibilities.

Canada has needs
I see being a citizen,
most are easily supplied
as those from other nations
continue to be the reminders,
those who choose us,
those somehow able to decide

to leave where War is,
to leave where their parents thrived,
to leave what offers nothing
for the children they keep alive.

Skin,
we are given in the beginning
when we are so little,
so brilliant our eyes
are the only colour
we allow to be any influence
to cause some loving commentary,
no reason for any dispute.

## MY PART, MY PLACE

I miss
so many in my life,
the People.

People,
who are my family,
my world-wide family,

who are
supposed to be
close family members,

the members
I think about,
I worry about.

So when the door opens,
(the border, perhaps),
the door to my part,
my place, I know

I am home, and those
I miss are never gone,
those who also welcome

the Syrians, the Americans,
all of the Everyones,
all of those who long to stay,
all of those who long to say,
"I too am home, Canada."

# THERE IS SO MUCH ROOM

A piece of fluff
comes on a breeze
to tell me something,
what it is I leave up to
the health of my imagination
I continue to consider a wealth,
something I will figure out.
A journey started at a tree
up on a branch where
Alarm sends messages from,
where the results of Wars
avoid the tales told by
news programs, social medias,
the smiling liars enslaved by ratings.
A piece of fluff on a breeze
comes to tell me
I must learn what I can
about fears only those
the War Mongers love to cause,
I must rise above so many
and understand Inclusion
before any acceptance of what
others around me believe
to be a useful stance,
a stance the future will reveal
as simply a form of what
the past suffered, a form of
knowing but not knowing.

## THE PEOPLE ARE WAVES
*for Lainee*

To be on one side of the window
is my gift at the moment
you see I paid for this
days away from the grind,
and by grind I mean
one thing for now, one thing
I know better than many,
one thing able to make me
feel the coolness of a wall
against my more-than-able back.

I have a job, too many don't.
I have an income, too many don't.
I have a home, too many don't.
I have a full fridge, too many don't.
I have a warm bed, too many don't.

To be able to open a cupboard door
and stand stopped by indecision,
to be able to sit & hear the cat purr
and enjoy a doc on Bobby Kennedy,
and finally know it takes Time
to present it, the gift called Duration,
the gift given to History, and it is
then Time's duration finally becomes
History, how the waves of People roll in,
and roll on back out, to only roll
on back in, the waves of People

I am watching, riding the waves they
find their lives atop, their lives somehow
riding a lack of food, riding a
lack of a job, riding a lack of an income,
riding a lack of a full fridge,
riding a lack of a warm bed,
to open the cupboard and find
themselves stopped by indecision.

And now, right now, this very moment,
to be on the other side of the window
and have that as my gift
what I also paid for, to be
part of another form of grind,
one which leaves a man standing
outside a liquor store,
dressed head-to-toe in camo
unable to shake with what was
his good hand, a hand
I sadly, yet gladly, place a fiver in.

# THE BROKEN GARDEN
### *for Doug C.*


Never mind the nightly or morning news
it isn't worth watching, or wasting
the time you call your life, to be
in front of the screen you pay too much for,
and finally say, "I have had enough of
Eden being a garden I am to tend,
Adam being some guy I must admire,
Eve being a leader of women somewhere,
and that poor innocent tree
with one branch some serpent chose."

I'll say it again, "I have had enough of
being called a sinner for the Cross,
for a Christ they have all wrong,
not a man I choose to see their way,
and all the Commandments used to
hold us back, keeping our humanness
from a fuller evolvement, letting minds
get beyond a book God had to self-publish,
had to rely on us to try to get through
without going to the mirror for a search,
a search of a face ready for some love."

Perhaps, I'll say it again, "I've had enough
of Christians, Muslims, Buddhists, and
the lot of you, saying this is a freedom,
what some of you may want to say

16

and may believe to say it is going
to provide a free pass to that place
supposedly under us known as Hell,
but, please, say it anyway, "I've had
enough of...", finally knowing to follow
all of those misadventures is a rip-off
devised and sent to leave you one thing,
the inability to hold out both hands
and help them from the many vessels
they had to board in order to sit
for the hours, hope held them within,
hours either upon a sea, or looking
at clouds constantly forming shapes
pointing at this country, our country,
and what you know to be a safe landing."

Regardless of all the heaven stuff
my worries have nothing to do with it,
as a member of the broken garden
if I ever go anywhere after my flesh is done
I ask it is a real place, one where
we all sit and hold hands screaming
a prayer to explode the War Machine.

## THE PRECARIOUS ADMISSION

*for the Asian man, 92, with dementia who was assaulted*
*at the store in East Vancouver, B. C.*

A man who once was a friend wasn't one.

So now I must make this admission:
Yes, I know a racist, him being
one of those justifying himself
by saying, "We must put Canadians first!"
But, really, in that, saying
"I am one who detests the Muslim & Asian."
And, yes, I say tell me, asking for
his definition of "Canadian."

So I also ask,
must I stand alone when speaking out?
Am I actually alone?
Am I really speaking out?

And I ask as well,
must I question what I stand for?
when a "maybe" haunts
what I once heard Bowie say,
"I stood for all a friend didn't".
Bowie singing a current influence.

And he, once a friend, has become
other than friend,
relying on silence to be the answer
to any question I have

18

sent via a current popular choice,
the questionable Social Media.

That little chat box where we
or perhaps, just me, came to know
who we aren't, what leads me
to now admit, resolutely myself,
"Yes, I once knew a racist."

# THE EXPANSE OF INCLUSION
*for Melanio*

All the blinds must be opened in the morning
in the home I never needed
to board an unexpected voyage to find,
to end up owning in a country
known around the world as Canada
where I would have to begin again,
finding enough jobs to finally
bring my family back together
after not being able to see my wife
and young son for the seven years it took
to watch them walk into the airport
near the town we can all call *our place*
where we will find lives both new & sane.
No, I never had to survive that.

To know how alive I am in the moment
comes due to his story of how he had to,
to begin a relationship with all things new,
things being how-tos, why-nots, what-ifs
or at times *should I stay or should I stay?*
And how alive I am in the moment also
can be gauged by never forgetting the sight
of his happiness and trying to imagine it,
only to accept I cannot, perhaps, just for now.
Yes, together, we chased a weekly pay-cheque.

Mel is short for Melanio.

Mel is short for Melanio.

A man from the Philippines,
who left his country before the foreign litter
was supposed to be a promise of
usable plastics, shipped by a saboteur
he even would have known as Harper,
shipped for the purpose of recycling what
is now being returned, an expense no new
man, no new taxpayer should have to pay.
Maybe, I too, want my homeland a difference.

There is no limit to any chance for change,
our so-called leaders no matter their errors,
no matter their unbearable duration in office,
seem to have an endless source of others
lined up eager to be replicas of them.

Some, then, ask why bother leaving homelands?
Some choose not to see and accept the reasons.
All I wish to say is *welcome* over and over!

# THE EROSION OF BORDERS

I cannot speak against the man
or show any allegiance
towards a far-too-old belief
he leaves his war-stolen homeland
to steal anything in mine.

I will not think against the man,
or stand with those fearful
of the amount of jobs available
he hopes just one becomes his.

I must not move against the man,
or try to forget the steps
into the shoes now on feet
he will wear to be a dancer.

How could I hate him
when he has his own dance,
has no fear about hugging
the men in his worried family,
even kisses them either
saying hello or goodbye?

I could not miss the chance
to offer a daring welcome
when he passes me on a street,
the eyes of his children
full of his indestructible promises.

# THE LIGHTING OF A CANDLE

It stands before me
still unlit
unlike the spreading problem
lit over & over because of hatred,
or am I wrong, am I afraid,
hatred is no fool, hatred is,
and I am not wrong or afraid
when it comes to what my pen wants.

I don't give a damn about keyboards,
or computers or cellphones, or that
unbelievable mouth called Social Media,
I give a damn about my country,
one known as Canada, one worth
giving more than a damn about, one,
the only one I have to give myself to.

The lighting of a candle
now bright, now lit long ago,
well maybe not so long ago
if I put aside any belief in time,
how it seems to be mad to pass,
to leave us another confusion as to
why it passes by day after day
in such an inexplicable hurry.

Please understand our world is not small,
meaning there is room, so much room
for one family, all the families who need
to escape what they call danger, what
we would call a report on the nightly news,
what I need to call an invitation,
"Please come to my country, you know
it is known as Canada, so many have come
before you, families, children, man & woman,
who stand somewhere with one match,
with one ancient and simple faith,
the lighting of a candle
can be a beginning, can be
like when a child is newly born
and the world becomes borderless,
the world is found in each & every flicker."

## A NATIONWIDE PLEA, OR A REQUEST
## FOR FEWER MISLED BORDERS

What I see
cannot be disputed--
I am poet
in this mess called 2019--
I am poet
regardless of your boredom
or strange lack of support.

I don't come from
Ireland or Italy,
I don't long to be
from any other country
other than this one.

Remember, we are Canadians!
Remember, I see!
Remember, I am a Canadian!

Immigrants, migrants, refugees, People,
hold onto your longing...
the music in the mouth,
the words of an anthem.

Hold on! Hold on! Grab it,
the history gives you it--
listen to your poets,
let them have some respect,

let them in, hear their words.

## ENDING WITH THE SKIN

If I were to look in a mirror
to see what colour mine is
and all the blood dares to tell
it would be a beginning I began
when the words spoken to my image
sound like a promise made to
other than who my eyes really see.

No matter how ignorant I am
there is one living beyond the eyes
only too eager to stand with inclusion
and all the blood dares to tell
even though such a story isn't long,
lasting for the length of an admission
using the mouth to admit how I feel.

If I were to look in a mirror
to see the colour of what encases me,
yes, may you see it too, I want that,
a mouth in the mirror to be yours
speaking of our imperfect planet
sputtering and spinning in this 21st century.

I embrace the voice speaking for all people,
for those asking to find the handy mirror
to look at themselves, and also
to see the others coming now, to be
in front of their new or first mirrors,
and like everyone should

when sizing themselves up,
be willing, left with a sort of smiling,
caused by finally seeing the self
hopefully ending with the skin,
and we, then, welcome each and every colour.

# THE CONTAMINATION OF RED

When the crowd is gathered
and I happen to be on the hill
it is then I can see all of
what the Smart TV has captured,
what I must say to myself
is a crowd gathered for worship
strangely made up of ties and ball-caps
all of them worn for worship,
a choice to begin the chant
loud in my mind instead of sleep
preventing me from feeling well
as the chant quickly becomes
the alarm-clock I never set,
a type of annoyance or disturbance
both dangerous and irresistible,
a chant going on and on like this:
*Trump is not a turd wearing a tie!*,
again:
*Trump is not a turd wearing a tie!*

A tie each time the crowd moves
I can see is red, yes, a red tie,
hanging from a neck, not hanging
the neck I often saw hanging him
in a dream, the *him* being known
by other than my dream, known
to be as red as the neck it
was around, or was it a *him*

28

who also sported a red ball-cap
with certain letters on the front,
letters I believe to be a lie
intentional,  sewn into that cap
to eventually reveal his need
to mislead, to ultimately be
what exposes him to be an
imposter, a flunky attempting
to play the role of president.

The contamination of red, yes,
the colour red, is taking me over,
I can no longer tolerate a tie.
I can no longer wear or watch
a red ball-cap, but the crowd
has been gathered, a crowd
made up of voters ready to
see their hatred illuminated
across the necks and foreheads,
a generation eager to forget
the peoples they put in boats
now heading for any port
Canada will wait at, waving
a flag offering a loving white
and a red still uninfected and free.

# LEARNING TO BE AN OLDER MAN

Sometimes the challenges our current world
forces on the days I feel settled
have little to do with the load
my new bones carry, meaning those
I now contain since reaching 60—well,
that was the waxy number friends & family
had stuck in the tastiest of cakes.

I still wonder if a singer wants the
audience to appear ready to hurt itself,
to be taking what he says & sings
as a point of ignition, any reason to
begin the circles to form a mosh-pit.

I still wonder where all my past
fellow workers, fellow partiers are,
now that this learning is under way--
are they in the same class, rooms or
lives all across Canada, no matter what
the years try to whisper each & every day?

As the yellowest leaves seem to twinkle
I long for a walk, with the season
we know comes before the snow, a freshness
the sniffling nose uses to revive me,
to remind me of the vein's health
during the steps toward brief breezes
also sent to be teachers as we
somehow survive another time of voting

when so many seem to be changing
due to how the world is sending them,
and, believe me, they come because of it
somehow still spinning, quiet orbits
regardless of the time clocks own.

Simply, how I may not be alone
with this new learning, this love of others,
those I eagerly await, others brought here
to our Canada I step back for,  stand up with,
trying to wisely & wily accept this Age.

# WHERE THE PATH IS MELTING

How quiet can a child be?

Please, please, bury me
with Hope Sandoval singing,
"In To Dust"
as the singer of Mazzy Star,
as the world becomes more bizarre.

How quiet can a man be?

Thank you, thank you, hear me
with only these words,
my words, no famous singer,
just me, saying these lines,
just the world ignoring the poet.

It is day now, so daylight talks,
in among all the voices of Winter
lodged where cold isn't a brute,
but when I recall that child
asking for so little when so little
I love how much I don't know,
I don't want to know.

Done with the branches' strengths
you come up the driveway
with perfect legs, playing yourself

through strings and power
left to a song you know I know.


The one left of where the pen sat, yes,
over in the drawer you protect
where the child & man have laughed
over and over because life gives
of course, gives each one a bit
of daylight and darkness.

Something someone will find
out in the middle of a field
where snow drifts over old footprints.

The melting path of all planning
to leave homelands being bombed
or lied to, taken from their children
they believe Canada can help raise,
can help to get to the other side
where a piece of clear ground is found.

No snow, no wind, no opposition
to them simply hoping
to stand and not slip on
any wish to have them fall.

# A RAVEN'S SERMON

An urbane couple united in more than marriage

wanders the weekend streets of Charlottetown

with many kinds of roofs partly wet and dry

enough to lift their exploring heads & eyes,

both open to not only the shocking nest

in a tree ready for the return of leaves

they could see as the shade soon to be,

how the stunning old church will stay cool

long after he & she return to lives in Truro,

the town known as the hub of Nova Scotia.

But it was the walk under that wild-tied nest

the way it sat so perfectly in the waking tree

like an unpacked family photo placed on

the corner of an old undusted night-table,

yes, the walk to locate a venue where poems

join the coffee and wine to entertain the minds

of a special gathering kind of feeling at home,

takes them back to the sight of the church, tree,

another home they now know the nest to be.


 And, now, when they think about all they can,

and those thoughts are about the homes they

can say have been homes, kind of where they

began knowing others are alive too,

breath allowing a life, those able to be

part of how their homes seem so far away,

high up in the memory, what may be a tree

there with a nest in it, a time when a season

could be compared to a town, city, province,

may even be a country, homes at one time

or another, inside or outside the memory.

Briefly, down below, both of them begin to hear

what in the moment sounds like advice,

sounds like a sermon they said went over well

when the church was in their lives, down below

a choice they hadn't made or found at that time,

when the nest seemed to be speaking to them

or the occupant covered in feathers unlike the

colour of the lone vocal gull, passing through

like some photo-bomb they both found hilarious.


In time their walk left them back in the hotel room

full of the sounds of the day and evening spoke,

enough to begin their own speaking, a conversation

made up of a quick need to reveal, to ask just once,

"Did you hear it? You know, when we were under

the nest in that tree beside the church we found

old and so mysterious. You know, it was like

a voice but not a human voice, more like what

would be heard when, perhaps, someone who

was new to the Maritimes, a Canada to share,

speaking in such a happy and relieved, almost

unusual way about how it had been finding a home.

A new home, far from the one home others

somehow had to agree they must leave, try

to attempt another life, one they hoped would

one day simply sound and seem as beautiful

as two, better yet, four wings flapping, a rhythm,

a beat some people have heard at least once, or

in time, like the smiling couple, believe to be

a gift their travels have brought, travels unlike

the people they will stand beside, the people

for the future, waiting, like unborn children,

or even unhatched eggs.

## THE GOOD IN US
*for James Walsh, singer for Star Sailor*


When my passing through is over,
when a woman smiles as she cries,
when my country stops being involved,
when that involvement isn't about wars,
when my country is really a peace-keeper,
I will know the good in us.

As my living becomes a dying,
as a man cries as he smiles,
as my life no longer includes greed,
as that greed wakes up with guilt,
as my wish takes over all doubts,
I can know the good in us.

Our tears are caused by a voice,
our voices can never be just noise,
our routines own everything we own,
our homes do not need large yards,
our properties belong to unhappy strangers,
I should know the good in us.

To fall over the top of a piano,
to punch a clock in order to be abused,
to sit on one side of a dirty window,
to sip a blend of fine coffee and rum,
to cry when a branch sways slowly,
I claim the good in us.

The good in us.
The good in us.
I see into the troubled now,
and hear a song so loud
I wonder if anyone else
can hear it, no, I wonder
why it plays so loudly for me,
I wonder if all of you
also feel and believe in
the good in us, knowing
it is there if we want it?

# DEPICTION
*for El Jones*

As I heard the laughter become
the weeping
and the weeping become the laughter
all that the laughter
tries to hide,
no signs of the life lived there
I've always noticed
how dirty snow can get.

She was looking
for the page on the stage
fallen, taken when the wind sang.

A stronger time
I ask the door about
but it has taken too many knocks.

A stronger scene
I ask the window about
but it has taken too many closures.

A stronger unity
I ask the home about
but it has taken too many renovations.

Marry me to the sky
even though I married a woman.

We have to make the roses grow.

I saw a woman walking with a leash
around the neck of a blue shadow
painting the dirty snow.

The only thing meaning
anything to me at the moment
are the starlings preening in the sun,
in the snowy cedar trees.

When I watch them
and their remarkable hunger
as the feeder on the front-deck
offers a variety of adored seeds.

All of this version, this depiction
to be taken as the life I am living
where some of those closest to me
are eager, are willing, continually to
take a stand for what I stand against.

The lies about an uprooted Muslim family
and all the Muslim families
that have stayed alive to make such a choice
I have no idea about, and I believe those
closest to me have no idea about.

How to find Canada, how to believe again
it is where a freedom is rampant,
it is where it is worth what it takes

to rebuild the lives of those families
who somehow have managed to say,
"We can, and we will."

# I SPEAK

*Remembering Kenneth Patchen, but*
*written for those war and politics uproot.*


I speak
because I can
because I can use my voice
to support your choice to move.

I speak
because I must
because I must be a man
who holds out a hand & smiles.

I speak
because I will
because I will move away from
the voices against you joining us.

I speak
because I empty
because I empty my being
of a past riddled with subtle racism.

because I fill
because I fill my heart easily
with a protest many sadly turn into a parade.

I speak
because I walk
because I walk on the same planet

43

now the new home your babies sleep in.

I speak
because I see
because I see through eyes
unfiltered by any blinded minds.

I speak
because I know
because I know there's nothing naive
about the handshake I long to perform,
I long to perform when the future provides
your seemingly settled trembling grasp.

# I SPEAK FOR YOU

Freedom surrounds my life at the moment
bees doing their thing in white clovers,
laughter at a nearby picnic-table is loud,
a hot late-day sun turns leg-skin red,
the whir-like noise from the college cafeteria,
a microscopic fly's blood hit across this page,
freedom has the voice of a young Bocelli,
but I speak for you
caught between a decision I know
isn't one anybody around me ponders,
a decision to be the one who is a parent
pushed against what must be a final wall
by a war your family has never spoke for.
I speak for you
knowing thousands here where you chose
are quick to call you criminal & target,
are convinced they own more than they own
singing to themselves some acceptable version
of the anthem you sat memorizing so long
you now stand on guard more easily.
I speak for you
a little man with a threatening mind,
an intelligent citizen seated alone on a bench,
a Canadian willing to say what it takes
to help you resume being father or mother
freed from the ransom a war insists can be paid.

# I SPEAK AGAINST YOU

Even though you may be like me
I speak against you,
you who speak against them
saying they are taking "our" jobs,
saying they are stealing gov't funds,
saying what I hear as exclusion.

Even though you are not like me
I speak against you,
you who speak from what I hear
as ignorance, as intolerance, as
what sounds as if you're a racist,
but I don't believe all that
feeling strongly you are better
than all that--after all I am sure
you live a life open to helping others.

Yes, helping, not adding to their
plight almost hard to understand.

Yes, being available, feeling something
about the humanity in yourself.

I expect better from the Canadian
you expect others to admire.

Even though you maybe like me
you are not in anyway that,
you are like those I watch close
and listen to the reluctance

46

coming out from your mouth,
words, even though they hurt
and exclude, are of the lost,
are hardly what this country needs.

Change is a word too.
One which hasn't been
sucked dry, hasn't been
taken off somewhere, far away
from its unchangeable definition.

# THE RIGHTS OF ONE

### 1.

Hatred is a pregnant mother too
and I have become a tiny man
but not so small hatred gets anything
over on me, just one who is able
to love, one who recalls his mother
long after she was pregnant with
a baby boy who grew to take a stand,
who knew eventually how to stand
against hatred, especially the kind
he felt should be called subtle,
the worse kind of hatred, able to trick
the tricksters, able to take away a
simple ability to love, meant to be
a beginning for the rights of one, a
chance to grow out of this tiny body
and stand up to any lies & lures
by the liar sent & paid to steal
the rights of One, to say where he wants
to call home, a new home if he must,
someplace he like I would prefer,
after surviving the last put down.

### 2.

Theft is a fertile young father even,
and I become a tinier kind of man
with a big pen ready to run out of ink,
a reason to consider the stupid man

isn't anyone I want close to it,
it being all about a man ready
to leave a place hatred takes down
by the insistence of war & poverty,
& disease & torture & politicians.
All enough for the cowards, the
annoying upstarts, a young man
eager to misunderstand what the
rights of One will cause, will allow
the poet to make with proper words,
another tiny man growing tinier as
our time becomes just one day I
will again take a stand  beside
all those coming to our Canada,
coming to begin, coming to explore
for the first time, a human being
being completely no longer out
on the cracking limb, being no
longer under the lies, being able
to apply the rights of One to themselves.

No one takes our jobs!
Stop being so unearthly white!
And begin to honour your ancestors!

# THE SMASHED CELLO

I adore, I crave the time
spent in front of the television,
the Smart TV, for only,
for mainly one reason,
the time spent allows me
as a man time to suddenly cry,
a type of weeping I seem
to learn a lot from,
the type of weeping I also
observe when watching what
I hope is the truth,
people from the lands that had war
able to survive the battles,
the bombardments, the choice
to mystify me, a choice I
haven't clues about, in no way
can ever know, can ever
endure in order to go on living,
a life without my leisure,
a life so different from mine,
a life I see as the smashed cello
once played by more than one player,
the smashed cello all must see,
all of us here in Canada
playing what we can, playing
the roles of what money brings,
playing the notes of comfort,
all of us trying not to leave
our homes, knowing our homes,
being open to how life sounds
no matter the instrument, the

on-going force hoping to make
the simplest of music, a
music given by the smashed cello,
there in pieces in front of us,
pieces like choices to exclude or include,
pieces like hands
on the body of a future
some of us hope to inhabit soon,
pieces many lives are willing to board.

## THE PROOF IS IN THE PUPPETEERS
*for Michael M.*

Beauty is also found
in the arrival of darkness,
I watched as the clouds
became the new land
and dear, rainy Glasgow
disappeared beneath them,
it was then I remembered
my son, the one I don't like
to call step-son, the one I
have heard say he loves me.

And that has been enough
throughout all the years we
managed to stay alive here
in a country where the news
given to the public in all ways
he now as a young man of 19
finds impossible to believe,
a young man alive in times
glutted with sources, sources he
will not trust, a young man I
sit and listen to, hearing his plight,
hearing him asking for honesty,
asking me to accept his pure mistrust,
or is it distrust, or is it being lost?

How many living-rooms are open
for his calm, for him to sit
and look at me, sitting in my

beliefs about all of it, all of
what I can say something about,
so he has more than my face
looking as searching as his.

Just the sofa and chair there
holding us for those moments
when we were able to share
not only opinions and vehemence
but all the easy-to-discern lies
we both were being fed, and
unfortunately paying for in order
for all of it to enter the room
where we sat briefly, a room we
grew up in, a room now filled
with a world we knew was better
than we heard, a world we knew
to be the one being lied about,
a room where my son was able to
reveal his feelings brought about
by a look in my eyes too, a look
so vital we felt life very close,
so close the talk faded into smiles.

Humour is also heard
in the departure of silence,
I smiled thinking of Wales
how much I had left there,
most of the world's strife
and how I needed my wife,
the woman who gave me him
that far-away young man filled with
all what he deals with daily.

But the dismay right beside me,
the load I know we both carried
even though an ocean then
was between us, was more
than him and his young years,
a load I will try to take
from his shoulders, from his doubts
I do not wish to see there any longer.

A beauty and humour our lives
will go on with, our chats cannot
stop being chats, even though all
of the world we hear about isn't
always the world where we try to live.

There are strings attached to them,
strings being agreeable in the hands
of the puppeteers, old, too old,
men dependent on the corporations
they have misled for the benefits,
for the lack of creative abilities
on how and when to make their
tugs, their pulls, on each string
to somehow mean goodness for those
they desire to swindle, and continue
to leave my son without a direction,
a quiet time where he could get
behind the removal of anything
I ever let set in my pointing eyes.

Hope is also found
in the whispers of the ones

54

our bodies and doubts have made.
The meaning of us,
of all of it, in a photo,
someone will find one soundless day,
one, perhaps, in the future when
the word *people* will always be
chosen before migrant, immigrant,
or even refugee.

# BANDAID ON THE SIDEWALK
*for Graham H.*

One day how
the future may sound
could be echoes
of children's footsteps
overtaking the ears
on my oversized head--
remember, it is actually spring
when the ditches begin to sing.

Isn't it timely how
the sun lights up
all the white hairs
on a black sweater.

One day the
sidewalk looks wounded
all the leaves
dead in pools of rain
fallen weeks back
without a season I crave,
my feet need, covered up by
perhaps, the numerous injuries
left unseen like Nature's worries?

A cover up
maybe, but doubtful
as I am growing certain the "we"
has grown more
aware for some reason--
I guess I just want

to believe in you,
all of those who are children.

I have decided to
not peel it back--
already knowing
the wounds of the world.

Strangely the students
play recorders outside,
songs drift through
then I can't decide
when such sounds
become reminders:
I don't know at the moment
but quickly I hear
voices asking
to peel off the bandaid,
*peel it off,*
dares posed by
those who'll take over,

those who can never hear what I do,
voices saying we will help others
coming to Canada for safer lives,
but we placed that bandaid there
on purpose, to help our future, to
find those who know about Inclusion.

I want to peel it off the sidewalk.
I want to take it off the world.
I won't be the one man scared of wounds.

When will we evolve?
To be, simply, loving?
Who gives their essence to skin?
Are we so limited when colour must be sullied?

Remember, children have put a bandaid
on the sidewalk where I was stopped,
where I'd never believe hatred
is, could, or will ever be a fashion.

# DECLARATION FOR THE BANISHED

May they come,
come in numbers.
May they be safe
no matter the plight,
no matter the chosen route.

Our economy needs them.
Our hospitals need them.
Our schools need them.
Our cities need them.
Our towns need them.
Our children need them.
Our fears need them.

I have no problem
with anyone
from any other country
coming to Canada
to exhibit the cost of
wanting to remain
a human being,
a human
being allowed a
new chance to be alive.

There, I said it.

## THE FLAGLESS FLAGPOLE

Today I can't care about
the intrusive news of the world,
and I can't care about
the life of a younger man seated
beside a bench I enjoy as the finches
share songs with a sun I can't care about,
only use as a hope to warm the back
of my neck where the wind
remains cold under the collar
I leave open in order to not care about
the stranger walking by, asking
himself, along with the wind and sun,
"Do you really think I am stupid?"

At this point in the bike-ride home
I can't care about the chem-trail
left in the blue sky above us, an
us I want to care about
only if we begin to take the time
seated out in the open where
we can be seen, bald-heads, ball-caps
on backwards and forwards,
burkas, niqabs, hijabs, turbans, etc.,
all we use to adorn or admit to
ourselves this is who I must be,
this is what I follow, what I believe in
if you will, what I wear allows a
tiny look into the self I am trying
to keep sacred, but what I wear
is meant to hide nothing other than

what we all were told to keep hidden,
boy and girl, man and woman.

Today I want to care about one thing,
a longing to be a Canadian...
being born here, or having had
the courage to choose this country
and somehow find the way,
to eventually stay on some land,
some perfect selected property.
You will soon own, soon call
a piece of the planet your new home.

# THE SILENCE OF TILES

*In Memory of the Barho children, lost in a fire, February 19, 2019, Halifax, N. S.*

How a floor has nothing to say
is really about a lack of listening,
a lack of hearing, is really about
the accumulation of dust left
by a lack of human awareness,
or a floor that has been stepped on,
is really about how floors
are speaking all the time
with one wish to keep speaking,
but the silence of tiles
is to remain utter loss
only found in the dust
left by certain footsteps,
when I see how the sun found them
and allowed me to finally know dust,
finally hear how the floor
has nothing to say.
But, in some corner where light isn't
I quietly make out
the sizes of the footsteps,
sizes I see range from
small to a bit larger,
like the sun sent seven different ones
all looking as if some children
have passed through,
seven sets in all, I see them
left so clearly in the dust
filled with what appears
to be ashes, appears to be

what a fire would leave behind,

but I am left again with
the silence of tiles,
no voices, no eyes, no faces, no smiles,
not even a whiff of any smoke,
of a flame, of anything I understand,
other than more of a story I heard
coming from some device
turned on in the morning,
in a living-room where I am alive
and have to take on the news,
what I try to avoid, but
unusually find myself in front of
the screen hearing about those
who once owned the footprints
the sun and dust eventually allow me
to somehow find my eyes
are unable to forget,
are so small but so dug in,
like little lives do when
playing certain games inside,
or walking down the halls of a school
before a broom can erase their presence,
or any tragedy striking
where they knew their home was,
and knew it as some place brand new,
a safer place where they could smile
without fear, look up to see the flag
of Nova Scotia, and hear it,
perhaps clapping, or loudly flapping
like a flag, somehow, still about freedom.

## WATERING THE FLAG

I heard the plant growing,
our recent household purchase
a Dracaena, the plant growing
to provide fresh air,
oxygen, so I heard,
now resting in the sunlight
down on the floor of our home,
of our living room, a room
all the plants seem to prefer.

I heard the water being drank
almost as if the thirst
of our recent purchase
can't be sated, the water being
sucked up quickly right before
my eyes, quickly like rain
vanishing at the base of a flagpole
where the concrete is broken,
rain recently fallen
now watering the flag,
a thirsty flag, rain to keep
the white bright, the red solid,
and the maple leaf spread wide,
not withered, a flag well watered...

I hear a nation anxious to grow,
to remain a magnetic home for many.

## MESSIAH FOR THE MISLED*
*to Trump*

For some mysterious and freaky reason
today I feel the need to forgive America,
not the nation you mislead and disgust,
and not the whole country you lied to
but a need coursing through me
because I am a Canadian and you
took something very wrong upon yourself
to try a lie about my homeland
on the world ready to agree one bullet
would solve so much, just the one
finger on the one trigger--you know
how much you adore your precious NRA-
a gun in the hand is worth two in your eyes.

No one has your bible fully read,
many have heard the lame preaching,
your attempts to be both Jesus and Judas;
today I feel the need to slap or slay you,
what the world is stalled by,
or eager to uphold for Stupidity,
hasn't come round due to the presidency
the greed of Corporate Earth gave you.

Or has it come round each time you tweet
obey the lure of a social media you don't own,
nothing more than a lonely man at a keyboard
trying to make desperation sound like guidance,
trying to unbury yourself, a committed fool
dancing beneath the strings you can't feel
allowing each and every move you make,

65

yes, dancing, to the pull of the CEOs with
their pants full due to the laughter you provide,
all the time believing the media is your baby.

As I said I am a Canadian, so the comedy you
offer has become irresistible, another show
to tune into if I choose to enjoy the reality of
what a century must endure, what a planet
is able to withstand, but mainly, what a man
who considers himself sane, a man who is the
man I live within, goes on watching you topple
yourself each time that hole in your head
somehow manages to open to say something,
pretty much anything related to utter decline.

And to end this I must point a straight finger
at you to say how dare you prevent any peoples
from being in charge of their own lives
and deciding to choose America for a new home,
perhaps you need to turn your empty head
northwards in order to watch a real leader,
one who knows the value of opening the nation
he leads, not building a wall or anything as nuts
as the plan you came up with, but a simple show
of how easy it is to actually be a helpful human.

*in memory of Osip Mandelstam*

## MEGAPHONES IN A PARADE
*for Terry Paris*

Once upon a time in Nova Scotia
there was a parade known
as the Apple Blossom Parade
in the fine town of Kentville,
a parade many years old
held to honour the blossoms
each year after they appear
on trees part of the orchards
owned by special local names
part of the valley, a valley
each one of you must travel and smell,
each one of those trees adding
to the smell, a brief reminder
sent out to the air we need,
sent out through each and every blossom
during this annual historic event
when the streets were filled with
other families, none of which
came to be bombarded by
five men who crashed the parade
with megaphones meant to louden
their hatred, their violation of what
we as Canadians know to be
a great freedom, how the world now
sees us, hears us, trusts us,
five men is all it takes-- was enough
to once again attempt to take away
the chance to support those blossoms,
those trees, that Nova Scotian town
where I am sure arms and minds are

far more open to incredible opportunities
people from other nations and cultures
are bringing for our futures,
far more than the five men
more than likely born in this province,
one trying to benefit any type of belief
or movement meant to add more
than take away from our brief stay,
the visit we call life, while breath
enters & exits us all!

# WHO I MOVE BESIDE
*to the N.C.A.*


To be caught in a song
isn't anything
like being
caught in a poem,
to be caught in a scene
is everything
unlike being
caught inside a man
who watches, who watches
the decline of men
who I move beside
but won't allow their hatred
or any of their smallness
to move within me.
Yes, I watch the decline of men
by seeing so many oversized ones
dressed in whiteness, a skin
I don't share with any of them,
a whiteness they believe is above
the colours of others, is known as
the *national alliance of citizens*--
what a catchy misleading lie-led name
kind of like *supremacists*, or *neo*-this
and *neo*-that-- so self-conscious,
self-blemished, so many selfish selves,
the little fellas with big hatreds,
who I move beside, I move away from,
I need to see, watch, little minded
caught up in some renewed worship

of whiteness, white skin, white bibles,
caught in the throats of these faux messiahs.

Such names, *Donald, Jared, Andrew, Jason,*
*Doug,* and even *Stephen,* tiny white
overly visionless boys now given power
by the shallow corporate pockets, endless
succession of *CEOs,* all holding the hats
full of ripped strips of unlined paper,
each one with the scribbled name of
each of them, who we withstand today,
names written in blue, red, black, or gray,
ink that can never be white, the succession
who I know is waiting to be picked
out of that growing hat, who I move beside
unalarmed, unafraid, of that ooze
the open cracks in our country now allow,
trying to paint us all with the loneliest colour,
imprisoned whiteness so thick & tired
of the isolated little minds, men not men
able to wave their own skins & grins
like sly egotistic stints of leadership.

# THE ARMS OF A PALESTINIAN WOMAN

What am I watching
late summer mystery
above my home
in the form of a number,
gulls in a crazed flight
as if my mind can say
it is some kind of mating,
all of them there never before
or did I miss this
in years gone by, days too,
all of it leaving me
to think about another beauty
my head lifts for, my eyes
stay pinned by, a sight I
am stopped for, the arms
of a Palestinian woman.

She on a daily basis deals with
what the American gov't openly funds
a nearby country the bible promotes,
the precious Is Rye Elle, she
watches from a window left opened
on purpose for a certain dust
to enter, to end up on the arms
of a Palestinian woman.

I endure a constancy each night
as the programmed mouths begin
when a certain hour has been paid for,
the smile millions let into their homes,

let into their beliefs, the beloved news
they use to create who the stations
want & tell them to be, the channels
flickering on the arms
of a Palestinian woman.
She carries a longing left too long,
it has moved throughout her,
what war drives her to decide
when there is no need to hide,
she feels the hands of her children
holding onto the only part of her
left smooth, attractive, the part
some men see as beautiful as a
sky full of gulls come and gone
like the arms of a Palestinian woman,
moving in ways like wings
meant to be a mystery, not to
shelter her young, to be a
scene never forgotten, the arms
of a Palestinian woman.

# THE IMPORTANT MISTAKES

The old woodwork must be empty!

I keep chanting to myself:

"There is no low low enough,
there is no low low enough...
is there no low low enough,
low enough for a boat to dock?"

The shoreline where many have
said goodbye to a place of birth,
a house no longer the home
now ready to become a distance.

My one wish is to watch the foot
lift from where the wave ends
up into a vessel maybe safe,
where the sea won't need to board too.

If it possible may the decision
to choose where I was born, Canada,
be the culmination of what has
the memory being generous as it fills
all those others with their reasons
to sit and feel what is belief
in transport, in a presentation
of what the mind has paid for.

The money I always wonder
comes from where, comes out of

how many jobs are taken to pay
for all what are soon to be
the most important mistakes made,
how a decision may mean peril.

May have been brought about
by a war, a hunger, a life of
watching the family you're part of
stay where they believe is theirs,
not quite determined to face
what freedom has possibly promised.

Yet, in that vessel many look out,
look up, as if attending a sermon,
smiling that brief smile
and understand the plan underway,
those rocking moments
of profound belief on a pew.

## A CHOICE OF SHIRTS

The memories caused by a stain
I discover one day during options
the open closet door provides,
what I quickly tell myself is
freedom found on multicoloured hangers,
all in there now allowed a brief light
bright enough to disrupt any choice
and bring about a new knowledge
I can call the most simple
or easy to understand:
there are shirts meant to be seen in
when an outing takes me into town,
or the one with the stain,
causing me to recall
former classmates & teammates
all part of families who came to Canada
at different times to avoid
what the world is still forced
to accept and accommodate
--people who hate, people who say
skin has the wrong colour,
people who leave bombarded homes
where they were born.

I have yet to give anyone the shirt off my back
here are, because of the stain,
the memories of those I long
to give my shirt to,
I pledge to somehow bring back
from a past so unlike

this neck-twisting present
I barely withstand,
here they are, each one I once saw
as only who I could pass the ball to,
who I threw stones at a school with,
who I won with when playing marbles
in the yard of Lord Beaconsfield School,
who I knew to be from Norway,
who I went on to hear was from Finland,
who I got the strap with
for throwing those stones,
who I came to understand was
being spanked far too hard.
who I survived certain classes with,
who shared his dad's 80 proof apple wine,
teaching me how to play Radar Love,
who became the one young woman
named Ingrid I shared explorations with,
who I knew was from Hong Kong,
who had three wives as
we worked at Xerox Canada ,
who would ask his wife to bring
samosas to work for lunch-break,
who came from England,
and over time became jealous when
I took up with a new friend,
who left Manila to be a father
and man seeking a new country,
who once stood in Northern Iran
by the Caspian Sea, each one brought
into my life at all the ages I once was,
each one I now take my shirt off for,
and stand very bare looking back

76

across who I managed to have
to help grow me into who I am now,
right here, right in the head, ready
to honour those whose families chose Canada,
some of the many shirts I have shared.

So let me do that. Here they are:

Domenico

I am sure you & your family came from Italy,
the certainty coming from
the clarity of my few memories of you,
being so Italian, being so good at
playing soccer down on that gravel field,
where your black hair is what stood out,
words I didn't understand,
when you wanted to pass the ball,
words I now know were ancient,
involved with where your family came from,
those words I know were saying,
"Move! Go ahead! Don't wait!",
but it was your hair I watched,
the black lure in the sun,
mixed with our uniforms,
along with how your smile told me
a goal is so, so, possible.
Now I understand. Now I know you, your family

RUDY

Today the memory seems dumb & stubborn
strangely I went to a little cloth bag

to remember how marbles and cobs
and steelies felt again, to remember how our
games were when the boys were wearing
Beatle hats and Beatle boots, even though
we were little boys playing marbles, and
the older ones cared more about their heads
and how the Beatle hats had to fit.
How it all was the Beatles
other than when I could flick
a marble over the schoolyard blacktop, with
one hope in mind, when I hit the cob I win.

Today the memory seems keen and kind
calmly letting your birthplace, Finland,
be part of what could be a brief confusion
about whether you had a brother named Ameil
or the other hand I see ready to make a shot
as those around us were all legs and 1962.

Our cloth bags were purple with gold letters
saying something about a drink we didn't know,
we only held in our cold little white hands
clenched at the top so not one marble fell out.
Both Rudy and his brother, well,
who I think is or was his brother,
always willing to exclaim
with an accent I found appealing,
an excitement I learned was no different
then mine, smiles go beyond
how the big world can be, go beyond
the size of a marble when the bell rings,
and we all must go back to a room
where so much is learned,

go on back up to the black playing court
designed for most to pass by in a car.

GREG AND GORDIE

An entire day is overtaken
by a rather autumnal scene,
how the wear on a petal's edge
has become how I begin to recall
friends who helped me put
stones on the street
for the goals we tried then
to flick the ball through,
friends with the last name of Swank,
and also Doerkson,
names coming from the Dutch,
coming from Austria,
and names none of us
then knew or cared
were part of families
and their histories,
better yet the choices
my friend's ancestors had
at moments when they felt
a move was the answer.

Greg, a Swank, wrapped in the skin
of his Dutch ancestors,
wrapped in the ripped Black Hawks jersey,
his favourite number on the back,
the number of Stan Mikita,
who certainly wasn't from any part of Holland,
one of his heroes who could've been from anywhere.

79

When the tennis ball became lost
even though it was so pink,  a colour
most would think easily found,
I seemed to be the one
who could find it
even though we all would comb the ditch.
I, alone, being strangely the one retriever,
bringing the pink requirement
for the game to ar and curse us.

I at ten years old loved Greg
until he chose
to say a number of hurtful words
about my mother already out on the deck
above our game,
simply hanging out
the wash of that day,
but I had to deal with
his words, words I took in,
I allowed to cause in me
the first time I ever swore
leading to my mother
hearing this first,
and ending our game,
demanding I tell
my friends to go home,
and get in the house right now,
so I did, and put away the game
heading upstairs for her words.

On other days, another friend,
Gordie Deorkson, who dedicated himself

to our road hockey empire,
stones or rocks found for a goal,
Deorksen, a name from some old tongue,
some old civilization perhaps no longer
with us, one that never had the chance
to enjoy dill pickles and grilled cheese
sandwiches, sitting with the television
full of heroes on skates with names like
Howe, Hull, Esposito, Orr, and Dryden.

Even though I said the word, "arsehole"
hockey would always be the sport where
faces didn't matter, faces with coloured
skin, none of that stuff mattered to us,
we only wanted a real net, bushes
we could find our seudo puck in
when one of us finally knew his
super-blade was curved too much.

## RAY MACKAY

Such a singer at such a young age.

All I remember is as his voice reached me,
is how much I then began to cherish the song, "Born Free".

All these years that continue to race by
stop in now, like some shocking visitor,
you know the one, but for me

this is about a song, a song returning,
how he sang it still leaves me wandering
the memories with such a smile,

tears in my eyes, a visitor
I wish was really him.

Is it MacKay? Or is it MacKy, like sky?
How that didn't enter my saying
you are a friend, we stood together
having no idea about the grades
before us, still purely boys
but part of the generation ready to
tap pencils on the covers of Elvis albums.

Now that I believe we are men—wait,
let me see if you're still alive, surely
the internet will say if not or if so,
my memories so not important to
all that my fingers type into the keyboard.
Ray, do you still sing?

I can still hear you if you don't
now knowing that voice came from
over the Atlantic where your parents
were singing songs about other freedoms.

LORNIE GILL

With middle name of Elvis
I had no problem
when I found out you really had it
and even better knowing eventually
you had a person of colour as ancestor
even though the little house
down from where I became farmer
had a dirt floor the one time

I was allowed, not invited, into
waiting for you, so we could head out
to stand in front of the pens
where the violent goats wanted us
to open the gate so they could land
on our shoulders, stop a myth
before we headed to the highway
in order to jump on bikes we loved,
both not knowing what was happening
as we mounted them to ride up
in a direction I seemed to know
was pleasing to you, a get-away
perhaps, to be far away from the
dirt floor, goat entertainment,
what your brothers expected you to be,
tough, sold to your mother smoking cigars
hanging out the laundry,
always loving your father
carrying the buckets of water as far
as he did, always being the father
you would see as the candles were lit.

BEN AFFUL

There is not enough love in my life
to tell anyone how much you
meant to me when we
made money for that Xerox place,
that Xerox palisade, you being
from Ghana, how I
waited for you to appear each shift
soon to know you had three wives.

Some smiles stick it out
over the years, some really touch
a spot in where some don't feel,
I never knew any type of spot
like that with you, feeling I
and you were well above
that job, our skin never
being anything that meant more
or less, we were men out in
a scene chasing a limited pay-cheque,

FRED "FRITZ" ROTH

I didn't need friends by then...
Osoyoos was not over the moon.

To make it after his phone-call
what mother forced to take.

When hatred is your first answer
to describe years under a father.

Grade 11 meant little when the farm
was taken from the farmer I wanted to be.

Becoming part of milk and cow-shit
became a longing I did have to leave.

In Osoyoos the beaches were close then
having made the move mother chose.

I didn't have a rubber dingy but
all the new boys definitely owned one.

The boys I didn't consider new
knowing they broke into the bakery.

Fritz, it was soon to be only your lure
even before I knew you played too.

I watched fingers on thin and fat strings
mine and his but quietly just his.

Fritz, I want to know if you live
so many times asking the computer if.

To find you again all the years after
we first drank your Dad's apple-wine.

How you knew the songs so quickly too
fingers moving on the SG fret-board.

The redness of that historic little Gibson
right there in the room we did have.

Where my father hated our exploring
how mono led so many to lead us.

But I stole the records we needed
fresh ones from within the plastic.

You were teacher without student
I didn't want to be a rock-star.

But the words grew within that
telling me to follow them forever.

Stopping the quest for inclusion in a band
opening the path to live somehow as poet.

EDDIE YU

What does one do with
a coworker from Hong Kong
who believes or explains
when urinating and the stream
separates to become two streams
is a show of good luck
and fortune will strike soon?

Aim straight at your floating life,
yes, in a dream I have had
seated at a meal with you,
with your young family, in
a booming sprawl called Calgary,
plates and dishes I adore
even in a dream where you
remind me of the split-stream
in front of wife and children.

We easily held positions at Xerox
eventual masters of refurbishing
a part known as the drum-mod
I believe took the customer's image
and copied it to a new page.

I won't forget you in green smocks
given to who chose their comfort,
how it fell from shoulders carrying

all the choices to leave a homeland
must've set upon them after the eyes
of your family agreed with yours.

Why you left I never did know,
no stories of how you made it here,
no talk of the shadows of stars
or boats loaded leaving docks
I could never imagine standing
or allowing a single human to leave,
all I have all these years later
is enough, you left why you left.

Today I can't find you anywhere-
no need to now, seeing how
I have what the past uses to educate,
the Canadian you helped me become.

## Mmap New African Poets Series

If you have enjoyed A *Matter of Inclusion* consider these other fine books in **Mmap New African Poets Series** from *Mwanaka Media and Publishing:*

*I Threw a Star in a Wine Glass* by Fethi Sassi
*Best New African Poets 2017 Anthology* by Tendai R Mwanaka and Daniel Da Purificacao
*Logbook Written by a Drifter* by Tendai Rinos Mwanaka
*Mad Bob Republic: Bloodlines, Bile and a Crying Child* by Tendai Rinos Mwanaka
*Zimbolicious Poetry Vol 1* by Tendai R Mwanaka and Edward Dzonze
*Zimbolicious Poetry Vol 2* by Tendai R Mwanaka and Edward Dzonze
*Zimbolicious: An Anthology of Zimbabwean Literature and Arts, Vol 3* by Tendai Mwanaka
*Under The Steel Yoke* by Jabulani Mzinyathi
*Fly in a Beehive* by Thato Tshukudu
*Bounding for Light* by Richard Mbuthia
*Sentiments* by Jackson Matimba
*Best New African Poets 2018 Anthology* by Tendai R Mwanaka and Nsah Mala
*Words That Matter* by Gerry Sikazwe
*The Ungendered* by Delia Watterson
*Ghetto Symphony* by Mandla Mavolwane
*Sky for a Foreign Bird* by Fethi Sassi
*A Portrait of Defiance* by Tendai Rinos Mwanaka
*Zimbolicious: An Anthology of Zimbabwean Literature and Arts, Vol 4* by Tendai Mwanaka and Jabulani Mzinyathi

*When Escape Becomes the only Lover* by Tendai R Mwanaka

وَيَسْهَرُ اللَّيْلُ عَلَى شَفَتِي...وَالْغَمَام by Fethi Sassi

*A Letter to the President* by Mbizo Chirasha

*This is not a poem* by Richard Inya

*Pressed flowers* by John Eppel

*Righteous Indignation* by Jabulani Mzinyathi:

*Blooming Cactus* by Mikateko Mbambo

*Rhythm of Life* by Olivia Ngozi Osouha

*Travellers Gather Dust and Lust* by Gabriel Awuah Mainoo

*Chitungwiza Mushamukuru: An Anthology from Zimbabwe's Biggest Ghetto Town* by Tendai Rinos Mwanaka

*Zimbolicious: An Anthology of Zimbabwean Literature and Arts, Vol 5* by Tendai Mwanaka

*Because Sadness is Beautiful?* by Tanaka Chidora

*Of Fresh Bloom and Smoke* by Abigail George

*Shades of Black* by Edward Dzonze

*Best New African Poets 2020 Anthology* by Tendai Rinos Mwanaka, Lorna Telma Zita and Balddine Moussa

*This Body is an Empty Vessel* by Beaton Galafa

*Between Places* by Tendai Rinos Mwanaka

*Zimbolicious: An Anthology of Zimbabwean Literature and Arts, Vol 6* by Tendai Mwanaka and Chenjerai Mhondera

*Best New African Poets 2021 Anthology* by Tendai Rinos Mwanaka, Lorna Telma Zita and Balddine Moussa

سِجِلٌّ مَكْتُوبٌ لِثَائِهِ by Tendai Rinos Mwanaka


**Soon to be released**

*Keeping the Sun Secret* by Marial Awendit

89

*Denga reshiri yokunze kwenyika* by Fethi Sassi

https://facebook.com/MwanakaMediaAndPublishing/

Printed in the United States
by Baker & Taylor Publisher Services